CW01508329

NORMANDY 44
German helmets

Dan TYLISZ

HISTOIRE & COLLECTIONS

Introduction

The new model steel helmet of 2 June 1935 was the symbol of a growing German army... It was the end result of improvements made to its 1916 predecessor and radiated the image of a new force within an old Europe whose armaments and tactics had become obsolete.

Approximately 25 million steel helmets (*Stahlhelme*) were made throughout the conflict for the forces of the Third Reich. The shell weighed between 810 and 1.130 grams depending on its size, and was made by five different manufacturers, the code of which was stamped underneath the edge of the helmet:

  – *ET/CKL:* Eisenhüttenwerke, in Thale,
  – *NS:* Vereinigte Deutsche Nickelwerke, in Schwerte
  – *HKP/SE*: Sächsiche Emaillier und Stanzwerke, in Lauter
  – *FS/EF*: A.G. Emaillierwerke Fulda
  – *Q*: Quist of Esslingen (who manufactured the 1940 Model until the end of the war).

There are five known liner manufacturers.

The smooth semi-matte paints applied in the factory in peacetime – colours ranging from a dull 'apple' green to a brighter hue – often acquired lustre with age. A great number of pre-war manufactured helmets were refurbished in March 1940 with the new slate gray dull and grainy finish. At the same time, the black-red-black Wappenschild decal introduced on 25 June 1935 was painted over, and omitted from newly made helmets. The

Hoheitszabzeichen (Heer eagle decal) remained on Army helmets until 28 August 1943. There are several variants of this decal, the early thin gray lines of early insignia being replaced by black lines, notwithstanding differences in the eagle itself (beak, feathers, claws and swastika).

There is sometimes a *Beschaffungsamt für Heer und Marine* oval acceptance ink stamp inside the shell which includes a date. This stamp, which is often seen on early production helmets, was less common afterwards, but it is sometimes seen on some Model 1940/42 helmets. Throughout the ten years of its existence, the materials used in the manufacture of the helmet underwent modifications due to economic reasons.

The parachutist helmet

A specific Model for airborne troops was adopted in June 1938. Its 1.15 mm thick shell was designed to resist impacts of up to 220 grams per mm^2 and was treated with manganese, carbon and chrome. It came in three sizes (66, 68 and 71) that could fit head sizes of between 53 and 61 cm. The manufacture of all the shells is traditionally attributed to ET/CKL, the code of which is cold stamped inside near the rim. However, the author can confirm that some Model 1938 shells were made by Quist, albeit in very small numbers. The shock-absorbing liner was made with an aluminium or zinc band ring solidly attached to the shell by four bolts that also served as ventilation.

The smooth natural colour sheep leather liner (sometimes pig leather) was in two parts that were stitched together lengthwise, with each one having two 25 mm and four 30 mm holes that optimised ventilation.

The shell had size and manufacturers' ink stamps, followed by, for early models, the stamp of the Berlin Luftwaffe depot (for example *L.B.A.B. 38*: Luftwaffebekleidungsamt Berlin 1938). From the end of 1942 onwards, a system of number coding was used (*Reichsbetriebsnummer*) instead of the previous manufacturer's markings, in order to hide the location of factories in Germany.

Seven rectangular rubber pads were inserted between the metal band and the leather liner, brown coloured for the first series, then in black synthetic rubber from 1940 onwards. Their thickness varied between 10 - 13 mm depending on the size of the liner. A wide piece of rubber padding was placed inside the top of the shell.

Model 1938 *parachutist helmet.*

Held in place by four bolts, the leather chin strap comprised of a friction buckle on the left hand side and a press stud on the right. Three aluminium (later zinc) grommets placed at the ends attached to the shell allowed for further length adjustment.

Once out of the factory, the helmet was given a coat of 'apple green' (a collector's denomination) paint for the early production models, then Feldgrau with the national tricolour shield on the right, as well as a second pattern stylised eagle on the left hand side, as was the case with other Luftwaffe steel helmets. From June 1940 onwards, the helmet was, in principle, painted with a slightly textured colour tone; the national tricolour shield was deleted.

Top.
Stahlhelm Mod. 1935
Rolled edge helmet, added air vents, aluminium band ring (strengthened in 1938), smooth 'apple green' finish, double decals of June 1935 to March 1940: national tricolour shield of black, white, red (Wappenschild) on the right, silver eagle (for the Heer) on a black background, left side.

Center.
Stahlhelm Mod.1935/40
Rolled edge, stamped air vents, iron liner band, generally rough texture dark matt paint, single decal of March 1940 to August 1943: silver eagle on a black background on the left side. This particular helmet was manufactured after mid-August 1943.

Right.
Stahlhelm Model 1940/42
Sharp edge, stamped air vents, iron liner band, smooth or rough dark green paint, single decal up to August 1943 (no decal after this date): silver eagle on a black background on the left side.
Note that a model without air vents was made at the end of the war.

Heer

In the first months of the war, army helmets were generally camouflaged by attaching foliage that would subdue the shiny smooth factory finish.

A bread bag strap or wire placed over the shell were also used to attach cloth covers. These expedients no doubt speeded up the adoption of a rough anti-reflective finish in March 1940. Later, even as regulation and locally made helmet covers appeared, camouflage paint schemes were applied on a large scale in all theatres of operations. These schemes were generally applied with care, with the helmet's owner, or whoever was given the job, often having to put a certain amount of thought into the design. Sometimes, the fresh paint dripped over into the inside of the shell and, although in general this area retained its original factory finish, a few rare examples show the camouflage having being extended to the interior.

The monochrome colours were, in the majority, applied according to the seasons and the theatres of operations. The paint was applied either solely by the soldier, or at unit level in batches and, as some photographs show, when the soldier was actually wearing his helmet.

Most common as a base colour for the camouflage schemes, the regulation tan colour was used on all fronts. The two or three-tone camouflage schemes are those most frequently encountered, but some helmets can have up to six colours. As well as the stripes, spots, mottling, square patterns and crosses etc., one also comes across imaginative and very 'artistic' designs that would have needed various sizes of brush to achieve. By using multiple colours, these schemes could rely on very complex geometrical shapes, replicating the camouflage scheme of the 1931 Model tent quarter or simulating leaf patterns, for instance.

Also, being in close proximity to a mechanised unit made it easier to use the regulation three colour scheme of sand, green and red ochre, even more so if air brushes from the workshops were available.

When this was not possible, civilian paints were used, resulting in colours that were too sharp. It was not rare, therefore, for a soldier to add his own personal touch by including an anti-reflective component. The latter could take the form of additives found in the field, such as sand, earth, wood shavings, plaster, grain husks etc. All of these could also be sprinkled onto the still wet first coat of paint, then painted over.

The use of wire netting over a camouflage base was also fairly frequent, one can also note that despite the 1943 orders to delete the decals on steel helmets, many soldiers retained the eagle, or carefully painted around it when adding camouflage.

Stahlhelm Mod. 1935/40 made by NS of Schwerte, found in Soissons in the Aisne, with a superb sprayed two-tone scheme of tan and green.
The perfection of this camouflage is optimised by the deliberately applied outline of the small mesh netting held tightly against the shell by a rubberised strap when the paint was applied.
The latter has left the factory green finish visible, thus resulting in a combination of three colours.
Note that the (Hoheitsabzeichen) decal has been deliberately covered by the paint.

Brush applied monochrome green associated with a texturing element on a Model 1935 made by EF of Fulda (N: 20767). As the soldier became more combat hardened, he perfected his camouflage by adding a rough anti-reflective texture. This was the result of mixing paint with elements found in the near environment. This was often covered by a second coat of paint. The Hoheitsabzeichen was protected from the paint by a mask.

This Model 1940 helmet was found in a small village near Alençon (Orne). It shows how effective the 'in the field' applied rough paint could be. Photographed in sunny weather, the green paint literally absorbs sunlight.

This Model 1935 helmet made by ET (N: 3892) was found in Belgium. It has received a very coarse brush-applied coat of dark green paint. The very high quality decal has been carefully left visible.

Mod. 35 *helmet that has been given a thick wash of white paint for the winter, even on the inside. The Hoheitsabzeichen has, however, been left apparent.*
With time, and depending on the quality of the paint, it is not uncommon for the white wash to take on a pink or pale yellow hue. This also depends on the paint base that it covers and the conditions in which the helmet has been stored.
This helmet, found in a Parisian jumble shop, shows the importance of the too rarely seen Feldpostnummer (army post office number), which makes it possible to trace certain 'souvenir' items to their original unit.
(Manufacturer ET: Eisenhüttenwerke based in the town of Thale)

Water-based white paint associated with a rough texture on a **Model 1940** *Stahlhelm made by ET of Thale. The shield was carefully protected during the application of the white paint.*

9

Single coat of tan on a Mod. 1940 *made by Quist. This paint, which was carefully applied with a spray gun, was covered by a large mesh netting held in place by six hooks. Note the grainy texture of the factory paint that conforms to the instructions of March 1940, as well as the care taken to paint around the eagle.*

This Model 1940 *Stahlhelm was found in Rugles (Eure) and has been daubed with tan paint, giving it a grainy aspect. (Manufacturer ET)*

Monochrome coat of light tan on a Model 1942 *Stahlhelm. From 1943 onwards, the base colour for German army matériel became tan. Naturally used for renovation in the field, it is, therefore, commonly seen on steel helmets, on the outside, but also on the inside rim of the shell. This regulation colour could adopt various shades due to the solvent used: water, petrol or oil.*

Three-tone colour scheme for this CKL made Model 42. One can easily make out a brush applied green square-shaped camouflage on top of the yellow base colour. The lower part of the shell has been daubed in a rudimentary fashion along its entire edge. The camouflage scheme is finished off with a few thin strokes of dark green. The Hoheitsabzeichen on the left hand side is almost invisible.

Paint gun applied tan base with long vertical apple green stripes along the entire edge of the shell. This Stahlhelm was made by ET (N. 3798).

Stahlhelm Mod. 35 with two-tone camouflage scheme, found at Saint-Pierre sur Dives (Normandy). A thick, messy green pattern has been added to the light tan base. Drips or fingerprints are frequently seen on visors due to the helmet being held there when the paint was still wet.
(Manufacturer ET)

The brightness of the colours used on this tan and green camouflaged Model 42 is an example of these colours' variations in intensity. This was due to various additives, or the use of civilian paints.

Note the dexterity of the owner of this Model 1940 in hiding the shield by spraying with green whereas he had obviously avoided getting paint on it when applying the tan base…

This Model 35 bears a two-colour camouflage scheme. It was found on a farm in the early 1990s at Naufles Saint-Martin (Eure). Green stripes have been added to the tan, enhancing the camouflage effect.
(Manufacturer NS. Vereinigte Deutsche Nickelwerke of Schwerte)

Spray gun applied monochrome tan finish on a Model 1940 Stahlhelm found in the south of France. It belonged to a soldier of Stab. II u. 5-8 Kompanie Infanterie-Regiment 933 (Feldpostnummer 24110 B). Note the outline of the shield beneath the stamped vent.

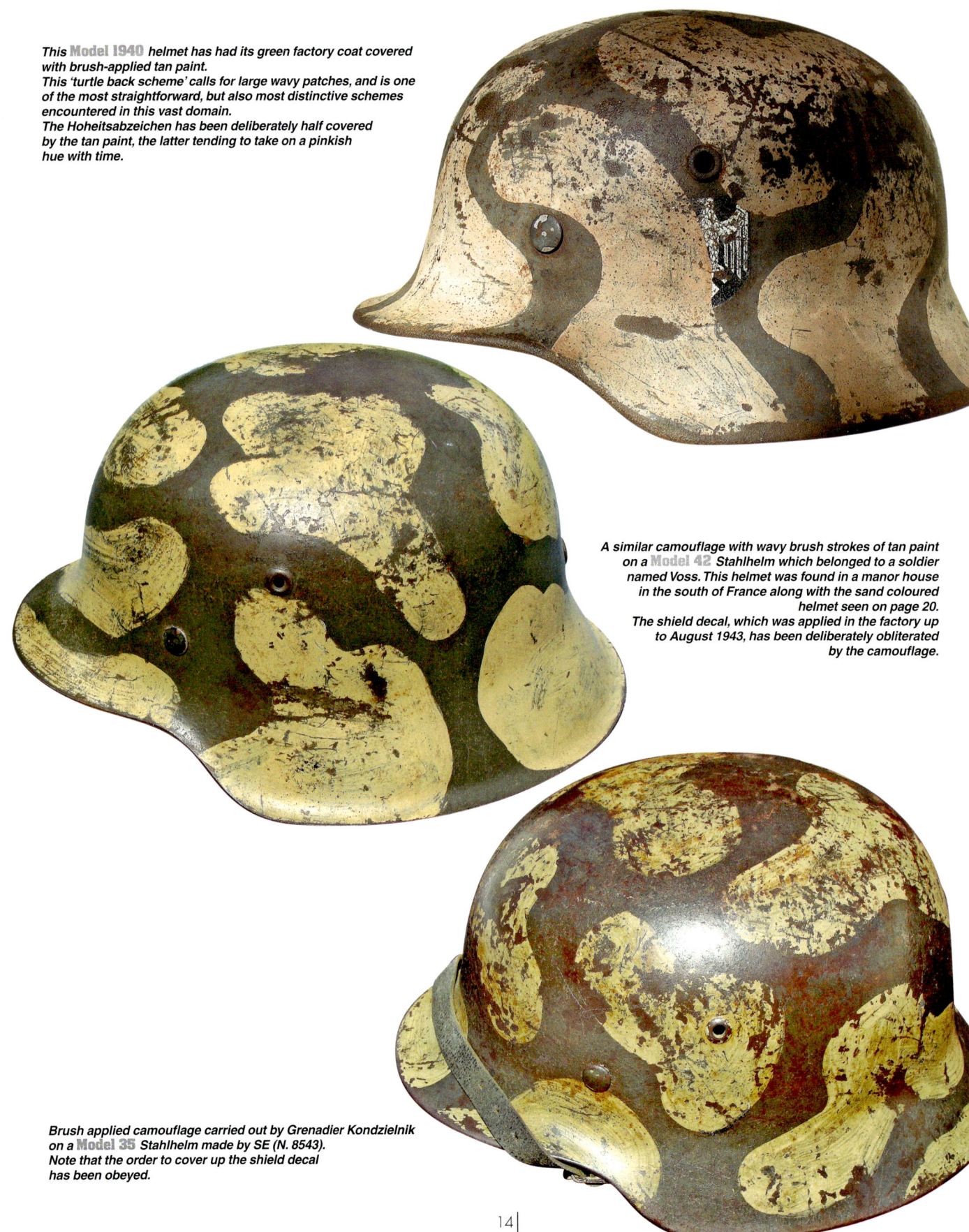

This Model 1940 helmet has had its green factory coat covered with brush-applied tan paint.
This 'turtle back scheme' calls for large wavy patches, and is one of the most straightforward, but also most distinctive schemes encountered in this vast domain.
The Hoheitsabzeichen has been deliberately half covered by the tan paint, the latter tending to take on a pinkish hue with time.

A similar camouflage with wavy brush strokes of tan paint on a Model 42 Stahlhelm which belonged to a soldier named Voss. This helmet was found in a manor house in the south of France along with the sand coloured helmet seen on page 20.
The shield decal, which was applied in the factory up to August 1943, has been deliberately obliterated by the camouflage.

Brush applied camouflage carried out by Grenadier Kondzielnik on a Model 35 Stahlhelm made by SE (N. 8543).
Note that the order to cover up the shield decal has been obeyed.

A superb brush applied pattern for this Model 35 Stahlhelm made by ET (N. 4723). This mix of tan and green is seldom seen with this scheme. The soldier who painted this helmet added a wavy green segmentation over a yellow base. The eagle decal has been carefully painted around.

Note that the silver varnish on some Heer shields yellows with age, and can lead to confusion with actual Kriegsmarine golden eagles (see example on page 74).

The owner's initials (HM) are penned inside the shell.

Model 42 helmet. The original green base colour has received green patches and stripes, completed by a few areas of pale green. The eagle decal has been totally covered by a brushstroke. The liner rivet sticking out from the shell is often indicative of a field improvisation, such as anchoring a length of wire there to hold netting or foliage.
(Manufacturer: HKP: Sächsiche Emailier und Stanzwerke based in the town of Lauter)

Another camouflage scheme applied to a **Model 42** made after mid-August 1943 (no eagle decal). The original finish has been covered with a sand base, to which the soldier has added dark green wavy stripes.
(Manufacturer CKL: Eisenhüttenwerke Thale. Note that this manufacturer was previously identified by the letters ET)

A typical example of the use of civilian paint on a **Model 42** helmet. No doubt surprised by the brightness of the green, the owner, a certain Karsten, added a few brushstrokes of yellow and ochre mixed with black patches. This is not uncommon with this type of camouflage.

16

A very nice example of a **Model 42** *which has been totally painted over with a tan base, only leaving the decal visible. Completed with a few strokes of green and red ochre, this helmet, which was found in Normandy, highlights the widespread use of this three-colour tone 'Invasion front' scheme in the West.*

This **Model 40** *with a three-colour 'Normandie' pattern belonged to a sniper who was part of a rearguard (three men) outside a small village near Avranches (Manche). After two hours of intense fighting, this helmet's owner was mortally wounded and his two comrades made a hasty withdrawal.*
Short tan and green stripes have been carefully applied to a brown base. Did this copy the geometric pattern of the Mod. 31 tent quarter, thus making up for the lack of a helmet cover?

Careful sprayed pattern on a **Model 35** *Stahlhelm (made by SE) found in Corbie near Amiens. The thin coat of tan paint has been embellished with wavy vertical green stripes.*

This **Model 1940** helmet has been swabbed with thick mustard colour paint accompanied by a few ochre stripes.

In place when the camouflage was applied, a length of wire placed around the shell is twisted around the liner rivets.

Found near Le Mans, this Quist (Esslingen) helmet bears the name of 'Stark' in white paint on the inside at the rear of the shell. Owner's names can also be found on liners and it is not uncommon to encounter several names on the same liner.

*Sprayed dark brown and green
on a brush applied light tan base.
This magnificent helmet, which saw fighting in
Normandy, also bears a small mesh netting attached by
two homemade hooks (the last one being a twisted piece of
wire holding it all together). Note that, despite all of the camouflage
measures, the eagle has been carefully painted around.*

*Three colour camouflage scheme on a **Model 1940** helmet.*
Tan base with daubed-on green and red ochre paint.
(Made by EF: Emaillirwerke AG based in the town of Fulda)

Model 42 *helmet with a five colour*
camouflage scheme.
Beginning with tan stripes, followed by green stripes,
the soldier who painted this helmet finished off by adding
ochre, grey and black patches.
The result is strangely reminiscent of the coats of certain cats.
Was this what the owner was hoping to achieve?

*Superb three-colour camouflage scheme
on this Model 42 Stahlhelm found in Laon (Aisne).
The tan base has been embellished by the addition
of short scattered red ochre and green stripes.*

21

Sprayed wide stripes on a Model 42 Stahlhelm in the classical
'Normandy' pattern of tan/red ochre/green.
The Hoheitsabzeichen has been carefully spared. We have noticed that many
decals have had their edges painted over, been half covered or just hidden
by a thin wash of paint.
Indeed, apart from the painstaking wiping away of wet paint with a finger
or a cloth, it is not uncommon to find traces of the protective mask
stuck to the paint. This leads us to believe that despite the orders
of 28 August 1943, soldiers often tried to keep the insignia visible.

Altough replaced by the Model 1935 helmet, the 1916 steel helmet
was still used during the Second World War. This Austrian-made
example was found at Saint-Gilles Croix-de-Vie on the Atlantic
coastline and has received the late tan/green/red ochre
camouflage scheme.

Spray gun applied wide red ochre/green patches on a tan base
for this Model 1940 Stahlhelm found in Saint-Malo, Brittany.

Another Saint-Malo found Stahlhelm, this time a Model 1935 with a brush applied tan base embellished with wide sprayed green patches and small red ochre blotches.

This Model 1940 (manufacturer ET) with a three-tone 'Normandy' camouflage scheme, found in the Sarthe, has a particularity. Indeed, one can see traces of adhesive tape on the tan base covered with wide green and red ochre stripes. Breaking the shell into two parts, these small stripes have been carefully applied along all of the front edge of the helmet.
In this case we cannot exclude the wearing of some sort of cloth item (a medic's armband for example). Could it also be an additional element reminiscent of the segmented schemes of German Great War helmets? The original factory finish has endured on the liner rivet heads, due to the quality of the metal. The original liner band on this Model 1940 helmet is made of aluminium.

23

This **Model 1935** Stahlhelm was found in Alençon (Orne) and as the perfect characteristics of a grainy textured helmet. The base tan paint was mixed with sand, thus forming a thick and rough coat. The soldier finished off the camouflage by adding green and red ochre patches.
(Manufacturer: ET)

A very effective rough finish has been brush applied to this **Model 42** Stahlhelm. It comprises of a thick coat of tan paint mixed with earth and gravel. Note that once again, the decal has been carefully avoided.

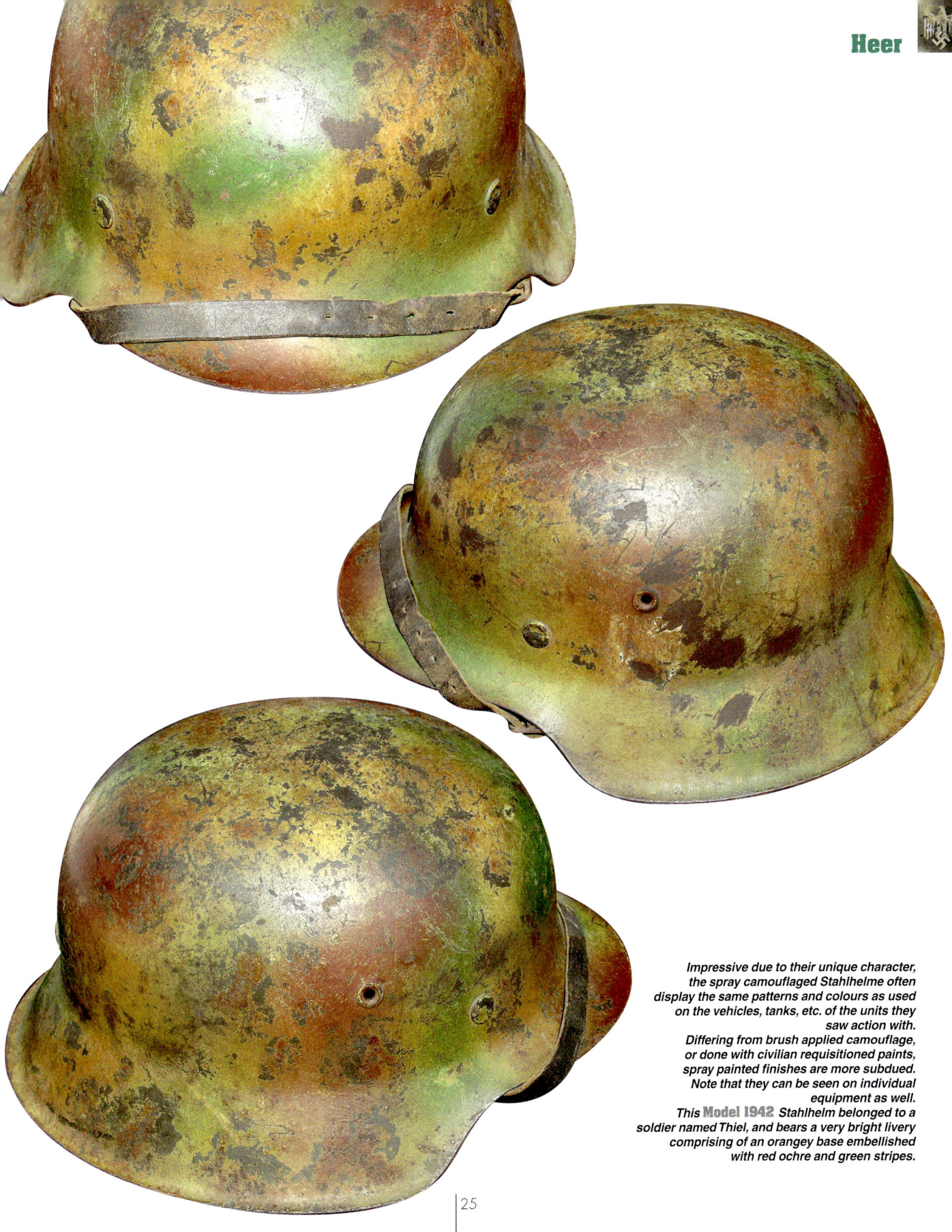

*Impressive due to their unique character,
the spray camouflaged Stahlhelme often
display the same patterns and colours as used
on the vehicles, tanks, etc. of the units they
saw action with.
Differing from brush applied camouflage,
or done with civilian requisitioned paints,
spray painted finishes are more subdued.
Note that they can be seen on individual
equipment as well.
This Model 1942 Stahlhelm belonged to a
soldier named Thiel, and bears a very bright livery
comprising of an orangey base embellished
with red ochre and green stripes.*

*A splendid alliance of blotches and thin stripes of tan/green/
red ochre that remain very bright on this Model 42 helmet.
The eagle has been left visible despite this strong
concentration of colours.
This helmet comes from the fighting for the Préfecture
de Police on Saturday 19 August 1944 during
the liberation of Paris.*

*Paint gun applied three-colour camouflage scheme
on this Model 42 Stahlhelm. The tan base coat has
been covered with red ochre and apple green patches.*

Practically identical to the previous helmet,
as much in the colours as in how they were
applied, this Model 42 helmet (made by NS) bears
a three-colour camouflage scheme of tan/red
ochre[1]/green patches.
Note the similarities in the tan stripes,
whose straight edges are perhaps due
to masking.
As well as the eagle which has not been
painted over, note the hook used to
attach camouflage netting.
The owner of this helmet was
involved in the fighting near the
Le Bourget airfield on 27 August
1944, when the 2nd French Armoured
Division, supported by FFI units, clashed with the
103rd and 105th grenadier regiments outside Paris.

1. Note that with these photos, which were taken outside late in the day, the red ochre looks distinctly brown.

Very carefully applied green/red ochre stripes on a tan base for this **Model 1935**. *The faded end of these stripes could mean that they were sprayed on. It should also be highlighted that it is not uncommon to see base paint that has been brushed on, then covered with other sprayed colours.*

Beautifully executed mottled three-colour pattern on a **Model 42:** *red ochre and green on a tan base. Note the brightness of the unusual shade of green, that is also seen on some camouflaged personal equipment. Thick wire for holding foliage was attached around the shell when the two colours were added.*
(Photos SS)

Very carefully applied camouflage scheme on this **CKL Model 42** *that saw action in Normandy. The pattern comprises of large patches from the front to the rear of the usual three-tone combination of tan/red ochre/green. Note the drips caused by a heavier application of the base coat.*

A **Model 42** helmet that was given a thick coat of tan coloured paint, applied from the front towards the rear of the shell. Note the marks left by the brush. The camouflage scheme is completed by stripes of green and dark red ochre. *(Manufacturer: NS)*

Very beautifully done three-colour pattern on this **Model 1940** helmet found near Toulouse. One can easily make out the clear outline of a large mesh net that was present when the wide green/red ochre stripes were applied over the tan base. *(Photo by SS)*

Pattern consisting of pine green/red ochre patches on top of a tan base. This **Mod. 1940** pattern Stahlhelm was found near Alençon (between Carrouges and Rânes) at the end of the 1980s. Note the outline left by the large mesh netting that was present when the ochre and green tones were sprayed on.

Another sprayed pattern on this ET made Model 1940 *Stahlhelm. The dark tan base is covered with red ochre and green stripes and patches. Note that the ochre colour has turned very reddish.*

Three-tone paint gun applied pattern on a Model 1935 *helmet made by NS (N. 6072). The tan base has been almost entirely covered by the red ochre and green colours. This is due to the fact that the paint gun nozzles were calibrated for painting larger objects such as vehicles.*

This Mod.1935 *Stahlhelm has received thinly coated and extremely bright, wide feldgrau/red ochre stripes on a tan base.*
A few chips in the camouflage scheme reveal the original 'apple green' factory finish specific to this model.
One can still make out the outline of the tricolour shield (Wappenschild) and that of the (Hoheitsabzeichen) adopted in February 1934.

Three-colour pattern on this Stahlhelm Mod. 1935, over an apple green base and consisting of more pronounced brown and green stripes. The scheme, as well as the colours used, is reminiscent of some camouflage clothing. The paint on the liner rivets has flaked away, this is due to the material used in their manufacture.
The rolled edge on the left side has been cut by a shell splinter.
(Manufacturer: ET)

Uncommon brush applied colours for this **Model 42** *Stahlhelm found in Gournay en Bray, east of Rouen. The green base is covered with large stripes of alternating tan and red ochre.*

This superb double decal **1935 Heer** *Stahlhelm sports the very rare early brush applied trio of orangey-tan/ brown/green as used by the pre-war Reichswehr.*

Left behind on a farm in Angerville-la-Campagne (Eure), this **Model 42** *helmet has a five-colour camouflage scheme. The tan base was later covered by a coat of rust coloured paint to which were added small patches of maroon combined with two different shades of green daubed over the entire helmet. The camouflage extends inside the shell.*

Very effective brush-applied camouflage for this
Model 1940 Stahlhelm. The thick pale tan base
paint was combined with a texturing material and
applied with a brush. 'Turtle shell' type dark green
geometric shapes
cover this. This disruptive pattern respects one
of the fundamental principles of camouflage,
that of breaking up a shape, cutting angles and
sharp edges.

Luftwaffe

As Luftwaffe units were often stationary for longer periods of time, one is more likely to encounter elaborate camouflage patterns that are almost works of art.

The flak units in particular held well equipped positions and their static role made it easier to develop their characteristic camouflage schemes.

Being stationed in the same place for long periods of time also encouraged the use of netting, paints and other materials found in the area.

As with Heer helmets, the colours changed depending on the seasons and theatres of operations.

The classic 'regulation' trio of tan/red ochre/green that was used on vehicles and equipment was also sprayed on helmets.

Civilian paints were also commonly used, as well as additives to obtain a grainy non-reflective finish. It should be noted that despite the difficulty, some skilful soldiers managed to avoid painting over the decals when applying the camouflage.

The frequent use within the Luftwaffe of the regulation camouflage netting, that appeared mid-war, did not mean that camouflage by paint became obsolete, but rather that the netting became complementary to this aim.

Also, camouflage painting was frequently accompanied by the addition of wire mesh, wire, 'ersatz' netting or rubber bands to hold foliage, grass or strips of cloth.

As there was no official directive in this domain, the ingenuity of the individual soldier resulted in unique helmets that were full of history!

Luftwaffe helmets followed the same rules as those issued to the Heer and the Kriegsmarine. However, despite the introduction of the Model 1940-45 Stahlhelm (made from mid-1942 to 1945), one can see that within the Luftwaffe, the latter was clearly overtaken in numbers by its predecessor, the Model 1935-40. This is no doubt due to the fact that it was not deemed necessary to re-equip troops who were often stationed far from the front-line. More up to date equipment was mostly destined for new units formed by the Heer.

Luftwaffe helmets were factory painted in a blue shade that oscillated between grey-blue and very dark blue (except for some rare feldgrau painted helmets, usually issued to ground troops such as the Felddivisionen).

These helmets bore two decals:
– the national tricolour shield (Wappenschild) of black/white/red on right hand side, up to March 1940
– the Luftwaffe pattern eagle (wings spread and clutching a swastika) on the left hand side, up to August 1943.

There were two eagle patterns, the first, which was smaller than the second, was used from 1935 to 1939 with at least four known variants comprising of insignificant differences. The most obvious

is that of a large swastika seen on early production shells. Other more subtle differences are seen in the tail feathers or the left leg positioned horizontally or curving upwardly (snake leg).

The second pattern eagle decal, which was larger and more styl-ised, was used on a large scale between 1938 and 1943.

A magnificent, rather artistic, extremely bright pattern for this perfectly preserved Model 1940 helmet found near Rânes (Orne). With two superimposed patterns of segmented stripes and compartmentalised red ochre then green on the dark blue factory paint, our artist has finished off his helmet by adding dots forming oval shapes all over the shell.

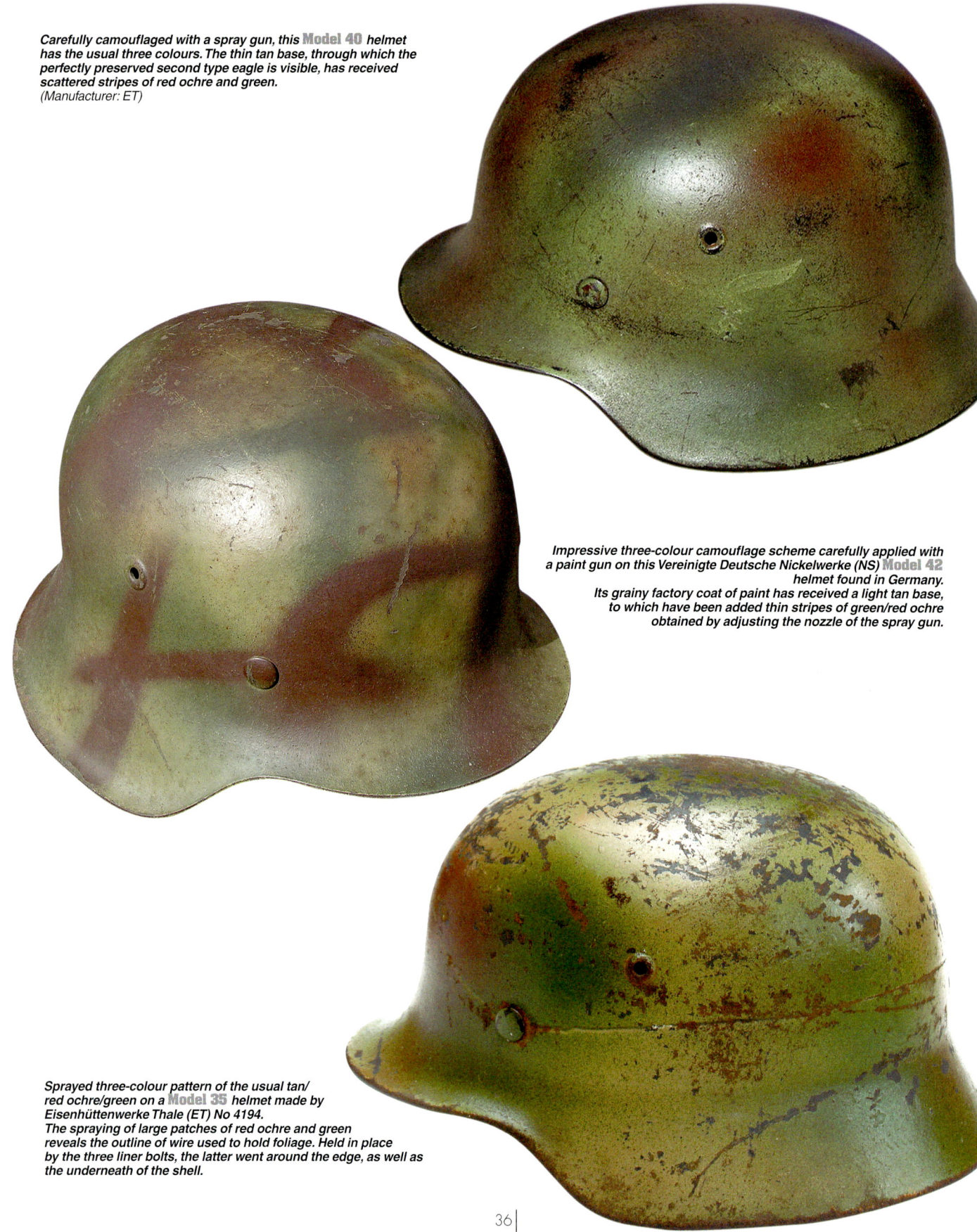

Carefully camouflaged with a spray gun, this **Model 40** helmet has the usual three colours. The thin tan base, through which the perfectly preserved second type eagle is visible, has received scattered stripes of red ochre and green.
(Manufacturer: ET)

Impressive three-colour camouflage scheme carefully applied with a paint gun on this Vereinigte Deutsche Nickelwerke (NS) **Model 42** helmet found in Germany.
Its grainy factory coat of paint has received a light tan base, to which have been added thin stripes of green/red ochre obtained by adjusting the nozzle of the spray gun.

Sprayed three-colour pattern of the usual tan/ red ochre/green on a **Model 35** helmet made by Eisenhüttenwerke Thale (ET) No 4194.
The spraying of large patches of red ochre and green reveals the outline of wire used to hold foliage. Held in place by the three liner bolts, the latter went around the edge, as well as the underneath of the shell.

36

Spray gun applied extremely bright three-colour scheme for this Model 1940 Stahlhelm.
Very large patches of green almost entirely cover the tan base and are embellished by small dots of red ochre.
The eagle pattern can be seen through the thin coat of paint.

Sprayed bright three-colour scheme on a Model 35 helmet. The tan base is covered with large patches of red ochre and green. A darker blue coat has covered the national colours (Wappenschild) as stipulated by the order of March 1940, only leaving visible the second pattern eagle, later hidden by the camouflage.

Very carefully paint gun applied three-colour camouflage scheme for this ET made Model 40 found in Normandy. The eagle is the second type. The intensity of the colours, embellished by large stripes on a tan base, results in a very bright finish.
As this helmet did not receive the grainy paint of March 1940, the colours painted on later lacked adherence and have started to come away.
Note how the soldier skilfully applied his initials AS under the rim.

Very rare *Model 42 helmet* with a feldgrau factory livery,
issued to Luftwaffe ground troops, such as the Felddivisionen.
The sprayed tan coat on the top, as well as the lower edge of the shell,
has left the second pattern eagle in perfect condition.

Thick brushed on shades of green/red
ochre on a *Model 35* Stahlhelm.
One can see the previous sprayed camouflage of tan and
green underneath. The soldier probably updated his helmet
camouflage due to being moved to a new theatre
of operations.
(Manufacturer: ET)

Carefully applied tan base covered with brush
applied green and red ochre on this *Model 40* found
in Fresnes near Paris. Note the presence of a second
pattern eagle under the camouflage, set over the
grainy finish stipulated by the order of March 1940.
The extremely good condition of the painted camouflage
stems from the presence of a regulation helmet cover,
adopted by the Heer in 1943.
The tan base has been carefully applied inside the shell.

Carefully chosen and well executed paint gun applied scheme on this Model 35 'double decal' Stahlhelm manufactured by Quist (Q, No 4808) in Esslingen. Wisely applied on a tan base and along the inside edge of the shell, thin green stripes (achieved by adjusting the paint gun nozzle) snake all over the shell. The camouflage scheme is finished off with scattered patches of red ochre.

Model 40 helmet found in the south of the Manche department. This type of camouflage varies depending on the intensity of the light. Indeed, the pattern of a tan paint over a green base gives it a yellowish hue in sunny weather and a green hue when cloudy. The cracks in the paint near the second pattern eagle are due to the amount of water solvent used along with the texturing material. This strong dilution is also seen in the white initials inside the shell.
(Manufacturer: Quist, No 6477)

Brush daubed four-colour camouflage scheme on a **Model 40** made by Sächsiche Emaillier und Stanzwerke (SE) of Lauter. An initial daubing of tan and grey is finished off by a duo of apple green/meadow green associated with a light texturing material. One can make out the outline of a wire netting for foliage around the shell and edge.

Very well executed sprayed tricolour camouflage scheme (tan/green/red ochre) where green is the dominating colour, on a very rare **Model 1935** which still sports both decals! The thin coat of green paint reveals the national colours as well as the first pattern eagle, rarely encountered on camouflaged helmets.
(Manufacturer: ET)

Spray gun applied tan base covered with large green patches on this Model 35 found at Sailly, near Fontenay Saint-Père. This helmet was without doubt worn by a soldier of the 18. Luftwaffe Felddivision that fought along the river Seine. The left side has received a very thick texturing material (wood shavings or grain husks).
A few chips in the paint reveal the presence of an eagle underneath the camouflage.

A camouflaged Model 42 helmet that has been given a very rough finish.
A brush applied green base, no doubt mixed with dirt, is covered with wavy light brown stripes.
(Manufacturer NS: Vereinigte Deutsche Nickelwerke, Schwerte).

A 'grainy' finish on this Model 1935 Stahlhelm found near Béziers in the south of France.
The textured finish is the result of a carefully made mixture of wood shavings or grain husks and tan paint, finished off with a few touches of spray gun applied green.
Pure tan paint was applied along the entire interior edge of the shell.

This *Model 1935* helmet made by EF (N. 20225) and found in the Champagne-Ardennes region, has received a sprayed camouflage scheme. Wide, light green stripes over the tan base have been embellished with red ochre patches. The initial factory livery of an unusual shade of blue, characteristic of all Luftwaffe Model 1935 helmets, has been covered by a darker coat, visible here in several areas.

Rough texture material has been applied to a two-colour camouflage scheme *Model 42* helmet. The use of a very bright shade of tan is no doubt due to the requisitioning of civilian paint. The camouflage is completed by roughly applied brush daubed green patches. The second pattern eagle can be seen under the paint.

This ET made *Model 1940* helmet was found in the South of France. It has been covered in a monochrome shade of bright tan.

42

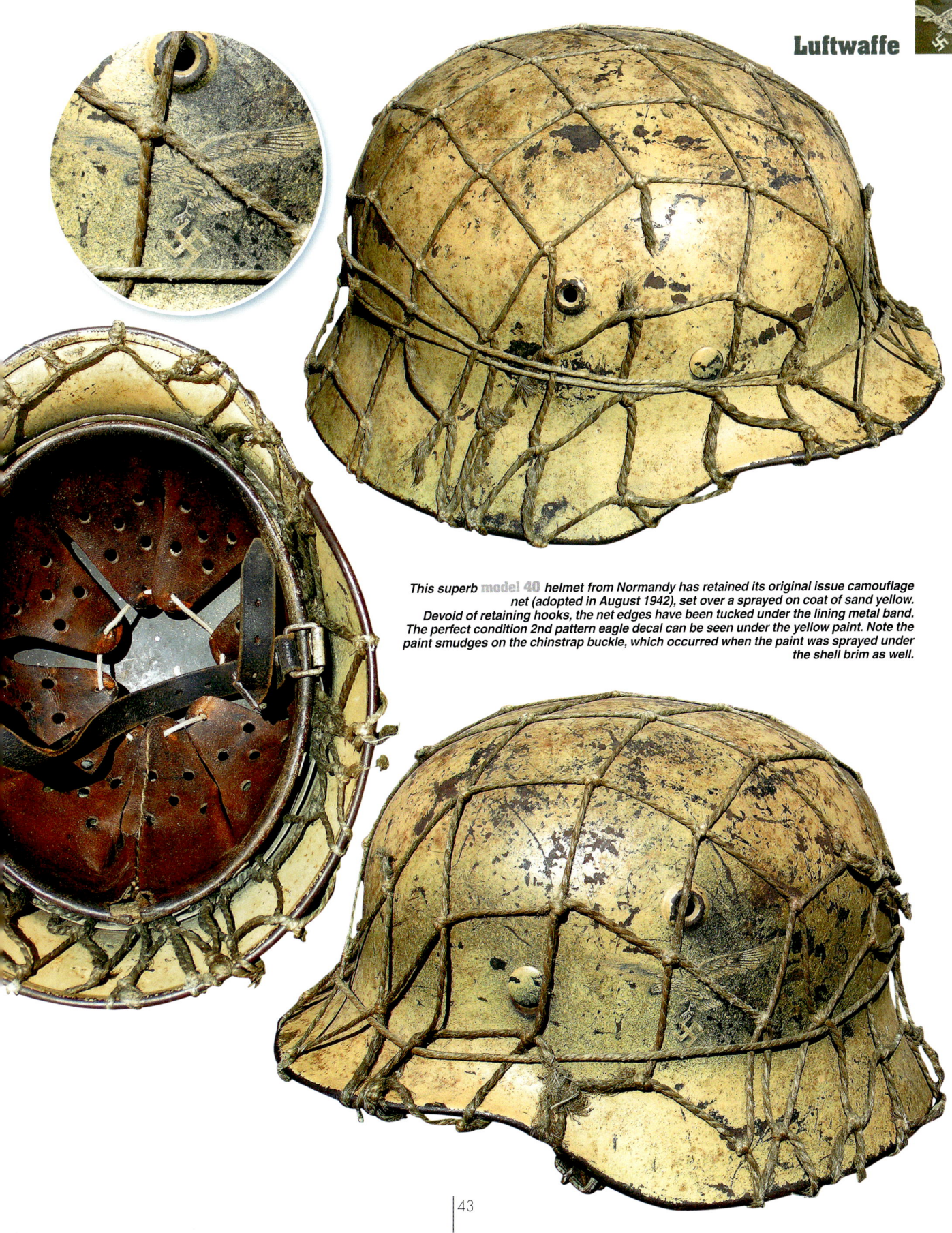

This superb **model 40** *helmet from Normandy has retained its original issue camouflage net (adopted in August 1942), set over a sprayed on coat of sand yellow. Devoid of retaining hooks, the net edges have been tucked under the lining metal band. The perfect condition 2nd pattern eagle decal can be seen under the yellow paint. Note the paint smudges on the chinstrap buckle, which occurred when the paint was sprayed under the shell brim as well.*

43

Impressive brush applied three-colour camouflage scheme on a Model 1942!
Deceptively straightforward, this pattern consists of adding a bluish paint over a tan base.
This is then partitioned by red ochre strips and finished off by short brush strokes of blue (spots and mottling).

Very carefully brush applied camouflage for this Model 35 Stahlhelm. *A very bright tan base is covered with wavy green patches. A view of the interior shows that the camouflage continues along the inside edge of the shell.*
(Manufacturer: Quist)

44

Superb brush-on scheme on this Model 35 found in the south of the Manche department. It comprises of a thick tan base covered with green patches. The trapezoid shapes are the result of the large mesh netting covering the helmet when the paint was applied. The latter, apparently made from thick cord used for hiding large objects, was attached to the liner bolts which were slightly loosened for this reason.
Chips to the paint reveal the national tricolour shield on the right side, and the outline of the second type eagle on the left.
(Helmet made by ET, No 3655)

*Magnificent example of very thick
texturing on a Model 40!
The large mesh netting was
present when the texturing and
dark green mottling was added,
it was later removed, thus achieving
a broken pattern.
The second pattern eagle has been
masked off during painting process
and is seen here in a triangular shape.
(Manufacturer: ET)*

*A similar textured paint
on this Model 40 with a
four-colour brush applied
scheme. The green base has
received large black patches
to which have been added tan
and red ochre.
Note how skilfully the second
pattern eagle has been protected
from this white texture, no doubt
some sort of construction material
(plaster, lime etc.) that has strongly adhered
to the factory paint.
(Manufacturer: Sächsiche Emaillier-und Stanzwerke, Lauter)*

*Thick, brush applied tan paint on a three-colour Model 40.
The impressive brush marks are highlighted by the sprayed
on duo of red ochre and green in long alternate stripes.
This texture has perhaps been achieved by applying brush
strokes to an almost dry thick coat of paint, either by the absence
of any solvent, or by the addition of texturing material.*

Superb brush applied scheme for this
Model 1935 Stahlhelm with perfectly preserved
national tricolour shield and second pattern
Luftwaffe eagle.
The shell is covered with short, wide stripes
alternating between the early colours of brown
and green. This helmet was found near Orleans
in the Loiret.

Sprayed on duo of tan/dark green for this Model 1940 *Stahlhelm (EF, No 1458), found in Autun, Saône-et-Loire.*
One can easily make out a second pattern eagle. The soldier's name (Friedrich Kratzert) is inked on the pig leather liner, as well as his Feldpostnummer. L-36639 identifies, from 28 April to 19 September 1940, Kommando Flughafenbereich Bordeaux and from 28 February to 29 July 1941 Kommando Flughafenbereich 5/XII.

Spray gun applied tan base with a light sand texture for this Model 40.
The camouflage scheme is completed by large green stripes and red ochre/green patches placed side by side. With paint gun applied camouflage, the texturing materials were always sprinkled over the first still-wet coat then covered by the second coat (for brush applied paint, the texturing material was always mixed in with the paint).

Sprayed two-colour pattern of large dark ochre and green patches on a tan base, mixed with texturing materials.
This helmet had a large mesh wire netting, the outline of which can be seen thanks to a second coat of ochre and green.
The second pattern eagle has been carefully left visible and one can see under its right wing the tan livery, uncommon for a steel helmet, and used for vehicles and equipment.

*Thick brush applied camouflage scheme for a Model 1940
Stahlhelm, comprising of a tan base accompanied by large
sprayed on green and red ochre patches.
Note the second pattern eagle which has been succinctly
outlined with a brush.*

*Paint gun applied camouflage scheme of large tan/ochre red/
green patches on a Model 1940 with a second pattern eagle.
Some tan and green paint is still visible on the chin strap.
This helmet was found in the Briouze/Fromentel sector
in the Orne.*
(Manufacturer: Quist of Esslingen, No 1837)

*Sprayed on trio of tan/pine green/dark ochre
on a rare Model 1935 Stahlhelm with a first pattern
decal. Chips to the paint reveal the national tricolour
shield which was deliberately painted over.*

Fallschirmjäger

In 1936, the Luftwaffe commander-in-chief Hermann Göring, ordered the creation of the first German airborne unit.

Formed for undertaking operations behind enemy lines, this new elite force underwent intensive training.

A first prototype helmet based on the Stahlhelm 1935 appeared in 1937. It was characterised by the lack of the extended brim and flared sides on the shell, the addition of a foam pad in the apex, and a special chinstrap that could be removed thanks to four spring loaded buckles attached to the standard Mod. 31 aluminium liner band (initially held in place by three fragile standard rivets). This first pattern helmet is easily identifiable by the slits near the edge on each side, for attaching the chin strap sections.

However, the final version appeared in June 1938 (see opposite page).

Often cut off in hostile territory, the airborne troops used camouflage on a large scale, not only on their steel helmets, but also on other elements of their equipment in order to help them merge into their surroundings.

Natural elements such as mud and foliage (ferns, grass, leaves and earth, etc.) were used to cover the helmet shell and complement the netting, helmet covers, as well as other types of locally made metallic supports made to hold foliage. Anti-reflection elements, either thin or thick, were used according to the theatre of operations, and then sprayed over. Depending on the individual soldier, these camouflage schemes were applied by buffing, daubing and/or glazing and can be simple or complex, as the photographs show. However, a straightforward pot of paint and a rough brush were often enough to add a monochrome camouflage scheme in the field! Other, more detailed, schemes required various sizes of brush, and comprised of geometric shapes such as stripes, patches, etc. This individual camouflage could also be used on the soldier's equipment, thus resulting in sets that were homogenous in both colours used and how they were applied.

As for regulation colours, here too, the massive use of a tan base on all fronts after 1943 was frequently accompanied by the duo of red ochre and green. Several coats of camouflage paint are sometimes seen on helmets and gas mask canisters, the result of a soldier being transferred from unit to unit.

Far left.
First pattern liner bolt (early production made of brass, then steel): the small holes on each side of the larger ventilation hole are for a specific spanner, ill-suited for repairs made in the field.

Center.
Second pattern liner bolt (aluminium): a large notch allows for the use of a flat bladed screwdriver.

At right.
Third pattern liner bolt (aluminium then steel): for this late production, the ventilation hole has been deleted.

Superb three-colour camouflage scheme applied on the Normandy front on a Model 38 helmet made by ET. The tan base paint has been mixed with a roughening texture made of wood cuttings and grasses. The scheme was then completed by large sprayed and blended stripes of red ochre and green.

51

An efficient daubed and brushed on shade of green over a tan paint, mixed with a thin roughening texture. The combination of these two colours retains its tone whatever the light.
The outline of the second pattern eagle decal has almost disappeared. This helmet that saw action in Normandy and which was found in Flers, in the Orne, sports a locally made aluminium wire foliage holder that was very popular on this front.
Note the 'apple green' factory finish visible on the inside of the shell (serial No 1783), as well as the rectangular ink stamp of the Berlin manufacturer K. Heisler, indicating the sizes.

Two colour camouflage scheme of tan/green mixed with a roughening texture on this ET made Model 38 found in Avranches (Manche). The second pattern eagle applied near a first pattern liner bolt is hardly visible under the paint.

Superb paint gun applied three colour camouflage scheme on a Model 38 made by Eisenhüttenwerke of Thale (ET No 5073). The pattern comprising of alternating slanted red ochre/green patches covers a slightly textured tan base. The second pattern eagle has been applied in regulation fashion below a first pattern liner bolt.
A view of the liner shows the aluminium band, the shock absorbing pads, as well as the 'Y' chinstrap that can be adjusted to three different lengths, guaranteeing a good overall fit. The liner manufacturer's markings (Karl Heisler of Berlin) show the sizes for a 61 cm head diameter, fitting a shell size of 71 cm (the largest).

The light green shade lightly applied on this Model 38 helmet is also visible on certain areas of the locally made foliage wire, held to the shell in four places.

Note the dexterity of the soldier when adding this wire, as evidenced by the twists. One can see the second pattern eagle under the thin coat of paint, positioned here once again below a first pattern liner bolt. It is not uncommon to find the owner's name and rank on the leather liner. Clearly written, or in abbreviation, they generally indicate the regiment, rank and name, here for 'Gefreiter Bonin.'

Two-colour scheme of tan and green on this Model 38 helmet found at Argentan in the Orne. A light texturing of wood chips was mixed into the tan paint. The second pattern eagle, carefully subdued by a thin coat of green paint, is positioned according to regulations below a first pattern liner bolt.

Another sprayed on scheme comprising of large blurred stripes of tan over the green factory finish for this helmet found in the Falaise Pocket. A rudimentary wire mesh is attached to the edge of the shell in four places. Note the heavy corrosion as well as the total absence of paint on the first pattern liner bolt, no doubt due to the poor quality of the metal used. The second pattern eagle can be seen under a tan coloured coat of paint.

An impressive camouflage scheme on this early production ET
made **Model 38.**
A brown colour has been daubed by brush onto a textured pine green base,
with the addition of a 'chicken wire' attached by four hooks.
Visible under a few scratches, the black/white/red Wappenschild has been covered
according to regulations. The only visible decal is that of the second pattern
Luftwaffe eagle, positioned below a first pattern liner bolt.

This beautifully applied two-tone camouflage of large blurred patches of tan and green has been embellished with a locally made foliage wire attached to the shell on four sides.

One can easily make out the second pattern eagle under a thin coat of tan paint. It has been deliberately kept clear, around its edges, of the light texturing material (wood cuttings or grain husks).

Paintgun applied camouflage of large green patches over a tan base with this ET made Model 38. The elongated shape of this shell, reminiscent of a turtle shell, is characteristic of large sizes, this one being a 71 cm shell adapted to fit a 59 cm diameter head.

A perfect camouflage applied by brush, with large patches of red ochre and green joined together over a tan base. The second pattern eagle has been carefully painted around but bears a few spots of tan paint. Decals were apparently wiped clear either with the fingertip or a cloth whilst the paint was still wet.
Scratches reveal the national Wappenschild decal (present on helmets up to 1940) on the right hand side. The liner bolts are of the first type.

This is how the regulation German helmet net, adopted in August 1942, would have looked, seen here on a Model 38 helmet that has received a thick coat of carefully applied tan paint.

This netting, issued with instructions, was held on the shell by a draw string with a metal ring at its extremity. The metal hooks were attached to the liner, one at the front, the other at the rear. These hooks were often unavailable or lost, and the netting was, therefore, tucked under the liner band or held by a rubber band or wire. Two small hooks held the extension designed to be worn over the face, when not in place. The netting could be used to hold various natural elements such as leaves, ferns, grass and so on.

A very light paint gun applied tan colour for this Model 38 helmet found in the Orne department. Note that the second pattern eagle with outspread wings has been carefully painted around.

A thick coat of brush applied tan paint mixed with a light texturing agent on this Model 38 shell, also found in the Orne.

A uniformly sprayed coat of regulation tan yellow on this *Model 38* shell found in France. It has been covered with 'chicken wire' to hold leaves, tightly secured to the edge of the shell.

A heavily blended three-colour sprayed on scheme
of orange tan/red ochre/green on this helmet found in Balleroy
in the Saint-Lô sector where the 3. Fallschirmjäger-Division
saw action.

For this very carefully applied camouflage scheme,
tan paint has been daubed all over the shell.
One can easily make out the jagged hole made
by a shell splinter on this helmet that was discovered
at Livarot in Normandy.
The second pattern eagle, positioned according
to regulations below the (third pattern) liner bolt,
can be seen under the camouflage.
This late production helmet is unusual in that
it has no manufacture markings stamped into
the inside rim the shell.

A very striking example of field camouflage
on a 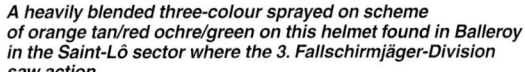 helmet with this pattern of large
brush-applied tan circular shapes over a rough
green base.
Note that this scheme seems typical
of the Mediterranean theatre of operations.
This late production helmet made by
Eisenhüttenwerke of Thale (ckl manufacturer's
code), has third pattern liner bolts and no eagle
decal, as stipulated on 28 August 1943 for all
of the Third Reich's armed forces.

60

*A thick coat of brush daubed tan/
green paint on this ET made
Model 38 helmet.
Note the traces of the two colours
in the twists of the 'chicken wire'
netting, as well as the deep marks left
on the shell, showing that the wire was
present when this very effective pattern
was added.
To further the splinter effect of the
camouflage, the chicken wire, held
by thick wire around the shell and four
aluminium hooks, could also be used to
hold foliage.
The second pattern eagle, applied below the first
pattern liner bolt is partially hidden by paint.*

Waffen-SS

The large scale issue of camouflaged cloth helmet covers within the Waffen-SS considerably slowed down the proliferation of camouflage on its helmets.

Due to its impressive capability of helping a soldier blend into the environment, the printed cloth used to make the *Tarnjacke* smock and the *Tarnbezüge* helmet covers was used until the end of the war.

However, the helmets of tank crews, generally hung to the outside of the turret, were camouflaged by brush or spray gun, at the same time as their tanks.

As with the other arms, Waffen-SS soldiers attached foliage to their helmets at the beginning of the war with the help of a bread bag strap or wire, they also used mud or paint to subdue them.

When the aforementioned cover was not available or not part of the unit's issue, the helmet was given a camouflage or not part of the unit's issue that varied according to the seasons and the theatres of operations.

The shields

On 12 August 1935, the SS high command decreed the use of decal insignia on the steel helmet. From that point on until November 1943, the right side bore a shield with two black SS runes on a silver background.

Up to March 1940, the left side bore a National Socialist Party shield consisting of a black swastika in a white circle on a red background.

It should be noted, however, that beyond these dates insignia continued to be added to the helmets by the majority of soldiers!

These shields were always edged in black, giving them, except for a few rare specimens, a slightly pointed base.

From 1937 onwards, a first variant of the runic was applied to the helmets, but the two designs were used indifferently on Model 1935/40 and 1942 helmets.

The Waffen-SS was issued with identical helmets, in terms of manufacture, to those issued to Wehrmacht personnel. Consequently, on helmets without decals made after mid-1943, only the presence of a Feldpostnummer (postal sector number) or the soldier's rank can identify him as a member of the Waffen-SS.

To conclude, we would also like to point out that a series of 1940 model helmets retaining the Party shield and runes decals was made especially for the Waffen-SS.

Although this order was earmarked for noncombat troops (such as concentration camp guards), the author confirms that some were worn within line units in Normandy.

A thin coat of paint gun applied light tan base on a Model 42 helmet made before mid-1943, found in the Manche.
A second light coat of paint partially covers the shield, revealing the second pattern runes.
The camouflage scheme is finished off with a few scattered apple green shade stripes.

This **Model 1942** helmet has been carefully camouflaged with a paint gun applied tan base and scattered green mottling. Despite the layering of the colours, once can easily make out the shield with first pattern runes on the right hand side of the shell.

Two-colour camouflage scheme on this Quist **Model 1940** helmet found in Belgium.
Note that post mid-1942 '1940 model' helmets (devoid of decals) were made until the end of the war by this manufacturer. Consequently, it is perfectly plausible to come across Model 40 shells with later pattern liner bands, without decals and sometimes with a shiny coat of paint caused by a scarcity of pigments/solvents.
A tan base applied carefully with a paint gun covers the first grainy coat and reaches as far as the inside edge of the shell; it is embellished by a few green patches.
As there is no shield, only the markings of one W. Borchert SS-Oberscharführer indicates that this helmet belonged to an NCO of the Waffen-SS.

This **Model 42** Stahlhelm, found in Ronai/Habloville south of Falaise, has received a monochrome sprayed tan coat finished off with large green patches. The shield on the right side of the shell has been completely hidden by the paint but its outline is still visible.

64

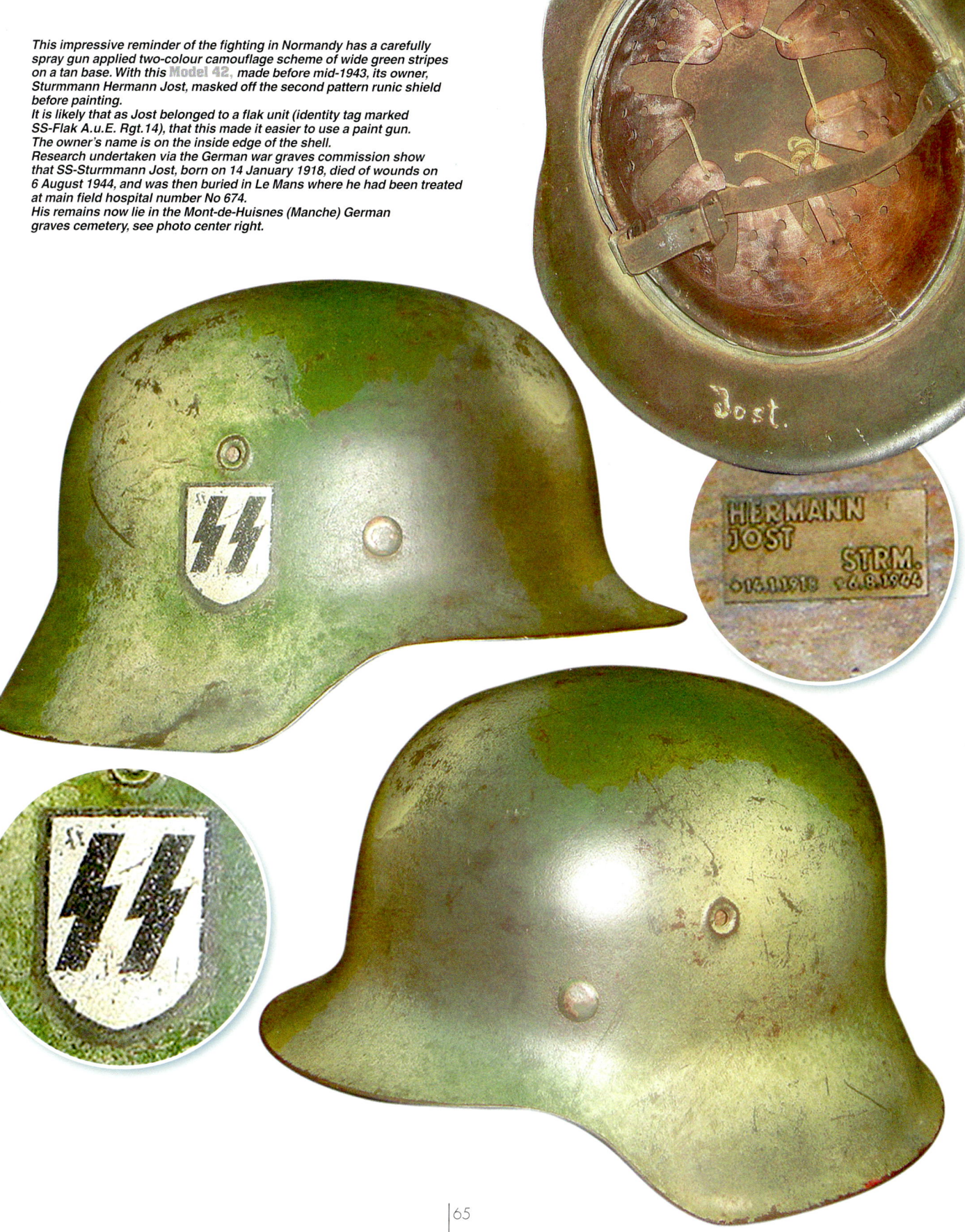

This impressive reminder of the fighting in Normandy has a carefully spray gun applied two-colour camouflage scheme of wide green stripes on a tan base. With this Model 42, made before mid-1943, its owner, Sturmmann Hermann Jost, masked off the second pattern runic shield before painting.

It is likely that as Jost belonged to a flak unit (identity tag marked SS-Flak A.u.E. Rgt.14), that this made it easier to use a paint gun. The owner's name is on the inside edge of the shell.

Research undertaken via the German war graves commission show that SS-Sturmmann Jost, born on 14 January 1918, died of wounds on 6 August 1944, and was then buried in Le Mans where he had been treated at main field hospital number No 674.

His remains now lie in the Mont-de-Huisnes (Manche) German graves cemetery, see photo center right.

Two-colour sprayed on tan/green patches and stripes on a *Model (made before mid-1943) 1942* Stahlhelm found in Normandy.
As with many similar helmets, the slightly grainy green factory paint has chipped away in places, making the first pattern runic shield even more visible, the latter having been masked off when the camouflage scheme was applied. The shell bears the stamped markings of SK 164 and 271C.

This *Model 1940* helmet from Germany has received a spray gun applied coat of white paint for the winter season.
This oil or solvent based civilian paint has been frequently painted over previous layers of paint.
Also used on a large scale to camouflage equipment, the water-based white paint, which could be washed off with water, has rarely survived on helmets as well as on leather and canvas equipment.
The thin coat of paint has spared the first pattern runes decal, on a silver background.
(Manufacturer ET No 6/9633)

Impressive daubed-on texturing of green paint on a *Model 1935* steel helmet.
Despite the complicated nature of this scheme, the soldier managed to leave the first pattern runes visible. The deep indentations in the thick whitish texture (plaster or lime) show that a small mesh netting was in place when the helmet received this camouflage.

Waffen-SS

Made by Eisenhüttenwerke (ET) of Thale, this double decal Model 35 helmet was updated after March 1940. These modifications consisted of covering the original 'apple green' livery with a dark grey semi-grainy matt paint, leaving only the runic shield, the one here being of the second pattern.
On this helmet, the decals have been uncovered after the application of the last layer. The helmet is finished off with a scheme of large apple green patches very carefully applied with a spray gun.

Sprayed on camouflage of large red ochre patches on a slightly textured shade of green. This Stahlhelm made ET, left behind during the Battle of Normandy on the outskirts of Trun, bears both of its decals, revealed by removing the camouflage paint.
Note the slightly pointed base of the first pattern runic shield, as well as the small bits of foliage stuck to the wet paint.
The Party decal is placed according to regulations under the non-stamped vent.

67

Very rare spray gun applied trio of tan/red ochre/green on a Polizei M.35 *Stahlhelm found in Troyes in the Aube department.*
Blended green patches merge into the light tan base and are accompanied by sparse red ochre mottled patches.
The thin coat of tan paint has left the two distinctive decals visible (these were used from 28 July 1936 until the end of the war).
The left hand side bears the police insignia (second pattern decal of a silver eagle on a black background and with a white border); the right hand side has the National Socialist Party shield.
Note that, as with the Wehrmacht, the arm of service decal is on the left side.

Model 1916 *Stahlhelm with two visible decals belonging to a soldier of the 19th SS-Polizei Regiment, killed when his armoured car was ambushed by members of the maquis at the Brive-St Yriex crossroads on the RN 20, twenty kilometres from Limoges. The brightness of the three-colour camouflage scheme is due to the use of a locally made 'oak leaf' pattern helmet cover.*
The eagle decal is the first pattern police type consisting of a silver eagle on a black background without a white border. Note that Polizei helmets bore two decals up to the end of the war.

Pre-1943 Model 1942 Stahlhelm made by ET (No J566) with first pattern runic shield. This helmet, belonging to a soldier named Höher, received a sprayed on tan base, finished off with large blended red ochre and green patches. This helmet was found in Martragny/Carcagny, near Bayeux. A local eyewitness stated that the helmet belonged to a Panzer unit that was forced to beat a hasty retreat from the village!

Very carefully sprayed on tricolour camouflage scheme on a Model 1940 helmet made by Quist (No T 2845) and found in the Lorraine.
The tan base is embellished by red ochre stripes associated with a very lightly sprayed on coat of green. The shield can still be seen underneath the paint on the right hand side. Note the owner's name Haug with a stylised H forming a double S…

Spray gun applied duo of red ochre/green patches on an ET made Model 1940 helmet.

Almost totally covered by a sprayed on camouflage scheme of wide red ochre and green patches, this Model 1942 helmet found in Normandy bears a neatly outlined second pattern decal. The helmet received a locally made wire netting after the camouflage paint had been applied, attached to the shell in four different spots.
Note that the front of the visor and the right hand side of the shell show small patches of tan paint, no doubt caused by the helmet being picked up whilst the colour was still wet.

Model 1940 Stahlhelm from the sector of fighting of 8-18 August 1944 in Bourg Saint-Léonard east of Argentan. The helmet is totally covered by a monochrome tan colour, leaving the first pattern runic shield visible.

Model 1940 Stahlhelm found in the Manche department: brush-applied green paint is associated with a texturing material. The camouflage scheme is completed with wavy dark ochre red patches. Note that the paint was wiped away from the second pattern runes before it had dried.

Three colours were sprayed on to this Model 1942 helmet made by Emaillirwerke AG (EF No 211). The tan base, covered with red ochre stripes, is embellished by a few discreet green streaks. Weakened by the adherence of the texturing material, small pieces of the shield visible on the right hand side have chipped away.

Kriegsmarine

Deployed on every coastline,
Kriegsmarine units were given the heavy
task of fighting off any allied invasion.

The fact that these land based naval units often remained in the same sectors, along with army units attached to coastal and port defences, facilitated the appearance of helmet camouflage, improved with specific accessories.

Indeed, the total absence of any official directives led to ingenious personal initiatives, which were usually carried out in small numbers.

The improvisation of string netting, burlap helmet covers which were sometimes painted, wire or other ways of attaching foliage with telephone cable, bicycle brake cables etc., showed how much the men wanted to blend into their surroundings (whether being stationed there long term or not).

Apart from the large scale use of attachment hooks, one notes that some of these improvised devices were held in place by liner rivets or by being threaded through the shell vents.

Despite the availability of materials used in the construction of bunkers and other structures, the use of texturing remained surprisingly rare within coastal units.

Monochrome shades of grey and blue were generally used by crews of ships engaged in coastal operations.

As for plain colours such as tan, white, green and rust, these were used according to the seasons and theatres of operations.

As with Wehrmacht units, the camouflage schemes using civilian or military paints (mixed with various additives) were mostly brush or spray gun applied.

As with the helmets used by the army, those of the Kriegsmarine had at first a green factory livery, but it should be noted that some were repainted in the factories with blue paint.

The navy Hoheitsabzeichen decal consisted of a gold coloured eagle on a black background, worn on the left hand side of the helmet until August 1943. Some decal variants have bright sparkling gold eagles. It should be remembered that some Heer decals, the varnish of which has turned yellow with age, can sometimes be confused with those of the Kriegsmarine.

The national tricolour shield was worn on the right side up to March 1940 and is very rarely encountered on camouflaged Kriegsmarine helmets.

As well as carefully wiping paint away before it dried, it was common for decals to be masked off when paint or texturing material was added.

Brush-applied tan base associated with a texturing material on a rare Model 1935 *Stahlhelm (ET, No4517) with its carefully painted-around double decals.*
The camouflage scheme is carefully finished off with a spray gun applied duo of red ochre and green.
The rank of Feldwebel and the function (Schirrmeister) are marked in white paint along the inside edge of the helmet. This rank could be the reason why the order pertaining to the painting over of insignia was ignored (apart for Polizei units).

Carefully sprayed on thin coat of grey on an ET made M.35 Stahlhelm found on the Provence coast. This colour could identify a crew member of a ship.
The chips to the paintwork allow us to see the various coats of paint on the shell, these being the green factory finish specific to the Model 35, as well as a dark blue commonly used in the navy. The gold coloured eagle on a black background has been carefully masked off before painting.

This rarely seen specimen has been repainted with a monochrome blue and given new navy decals. The inside of the shell retains the green livery specific to Model 35 helmets.
The owner's name and rank are written above the production number 4805 in the shell.

74

Very bright spray gun applied colours on this Model 40 made by ET (No 222) found in Seine-Maritime.
A sprayed on base of grey-blue covers the factory feldgrau and is streaked with tan stripes.
This camouflage scheme and colours were very popular within coastal defence units. The shield, carefully avoided during the application of the paint, is a first pattern gold coloured eagle on a black background, recognisable by its fine lines. The highlighting of certain details in a stronger gold colour is also found on refurbished Kriegsmarine Model 1916 helmets.

Very carefully applied camouflage scheme mixing tan and grey
on a Model 35 helmet found near Toulouse.
Large tan patches have been sprayed onto the grey base that totally
covers the smooth factory finish specific to these early shells.
There are two names written on the Model 31 leather liner:
Armbrecht and Barts.

An extremely well preserved spray gun applied three-colour
camouflage scheme on a Model 40 (ET). Large patches of
red ochre have been added to a tan base.
The new non-reflective factory finish of 1940 optimised the
matt aspect of the later camouflage, which blended into the
texture. This was due to the great amount of water used in
the mixture (this then evaporated allowing the paint to
adhere perfectly to the helmet).
Note the shield under the stamped vent.
A specific navy serial number (N 7518 S)
is accompanied by the owner's name
(A. Domann).

Very effective brush-applied mottled effect on a Model 42
made before mid-1943. The four colours have been mixed with
a texturing material; pine green/light green/dark brown/tan.
The shield, tilted when affixed in the factory, has been masked off, leaving
it clear of any camouflage material.

An efficient double colour camouflage scheme on a Model 1940 helmet found near Nice in Southern France.
Enhanced by the dull and textured finish introduced in March 1940, the light tan base has been finished off by deftly brushed on stripes of very dark green.
There is a previously applied bright blue paint on the inside edge and along the edges of the liner band as well as the chin strap. The name of the owner (H. Meineke) is done in black paint.

A slightly grainy tan base embellished with dark red ochre and green patches on this Model 42 made by Sächsische Emaillier und Stanzwerke (coded hkp). The gold coloured eagle shield was made visible whilst the paint was still wet.

Spray painted camouflage scheme on a Model 35 with large red ochre/green patches on a tan base.
Note the previously applied coat of thick, slightly grainy bright tan paint underneath, frequently seen in Mediterranean theatres of operations.
This second camouflage scheme was generally applied following a new posting. The outline of the eagle decal that was masked off for the previous camouflage scheme is visible.

A superb helmet found in Royan, Charente-Maritime, covered with burlap which has been sprayed with red ochre and green! The cover is attached to the shell by wire along the edges and is covered with large mesh netting.
Note that this type of cover was very popular with coastal troops.

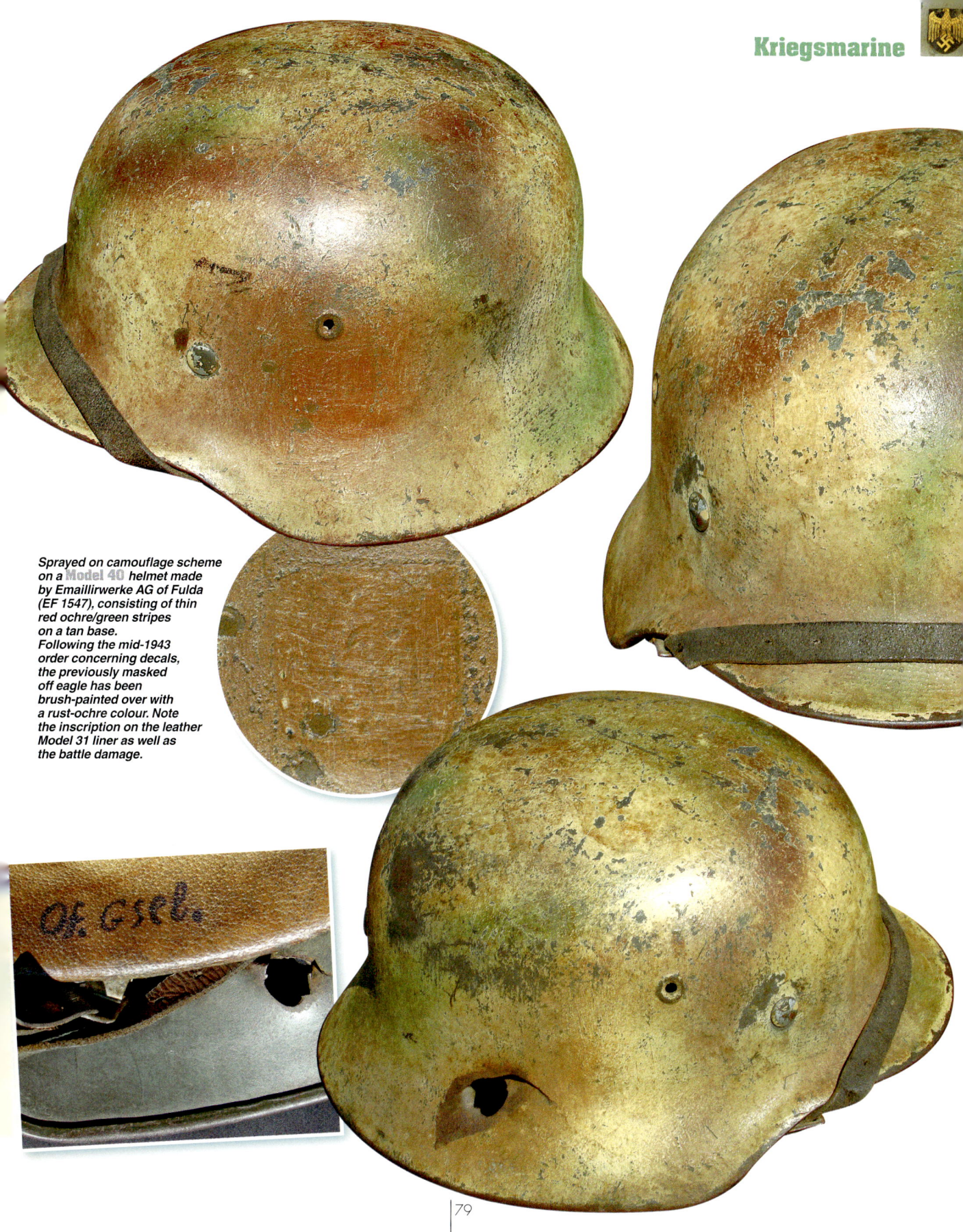

Sprayed on camouflage scheme on a **Model 40** helmet made by Emaillirwerke AG of Fulda (EF 1547), consisting of thin red ochre/green stripes on a tan base.
Following the mid-1943 order concerning decals, the previously masked off eagle has been brush-painted over with a rust-ochre colour. Note the inscription on the leather Model 31 liner as well as the battle damage.

Of. Gsel.

This brush-painted
Model 42 shell made before
mid-1943 shows a very pale
shade of green that totally
covers the outside and inside.
Note that it is extremely rare
to encounter the primary
camouflage colour inside the
shell. This pale green base has
been mixed with a texturing
material (sand/earth) and covered
with wide stripes of sprayed
on pine green.
The gold coloured eagle shield
has been carefully masked off.

Carefully applied anti-reflective paint on another
Model 42 *Stahlhelm from Royan.*
The green coloured base mixed with sand is covered with a
network of brown stripes which break up the shape of the helmet.

Superb and bright camouflage carefully applied to a Model 42 Stahlhelm found in the Aisne department.
The seaman artist has added red ochre and green mottling with a small brush over the brushed on tan base!
A few chips to the paint reveal the gold coloured Kriegsmarine eagle.

Many articles by the author have been published in the French monthly MILITARIA MAGAZINE available by subscription and from *www.militaria-mag.com*

Join the community of militaria collectors and military history enthusiasts on facebook
http://www.facebook.com/Militaria.Magazine

ACKNOWLEDGEMENTS

The author would like to thank the following for their constant support:
Arromanches Militaria, Alex, Alain L., O. Cantal, L. Charbonneau, Dead Man's Corner museum at Saint-Côme du Mont, Denis D., EB Normandie 44, Eric P, FK, the Goliath company, Hervé J., J-M V., A. Krause, Lionel P, I. Marchina, T. Monnier, E. and M. Monbel, MP, Olivier M., Peter from Militaria.fr, B. Renoux, Richard R., D. Stradella, S. Sans, J. Saddier, N. Valois, E. Waltersperger, as well as many other private collectors.

This book was edited by Philippe Charbonnier.
Design and layout Matthieu Pleissinger and Gil Bourdeaux.
Translated from the french by Lawrence Brown.

Histoire & Collections
SA au capital de 182 938,82 €
5, avenue de la République
F-75541 Paris Cédex 11
Tel : +33-1 40 21 18 20 / Fax : +33-1 47 00 51 11
www.histoireetcollections.com

This book has been designed, typed, laid-out and processed by *Histoire & Collections* on fully integrated computer equipment.
Color separation: *Studio A&C*
Printed by ZURE.
Spain, European Union.
September 2011.